# What ha

I had an accident    2

The ambulance    4

At the hospital    6

Six weeks later    8

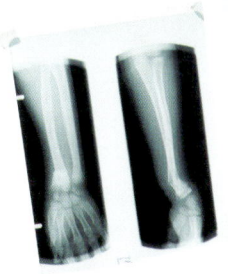

# I had an accident

I fell off my swing.

My arm was very sore.

# The ambulance

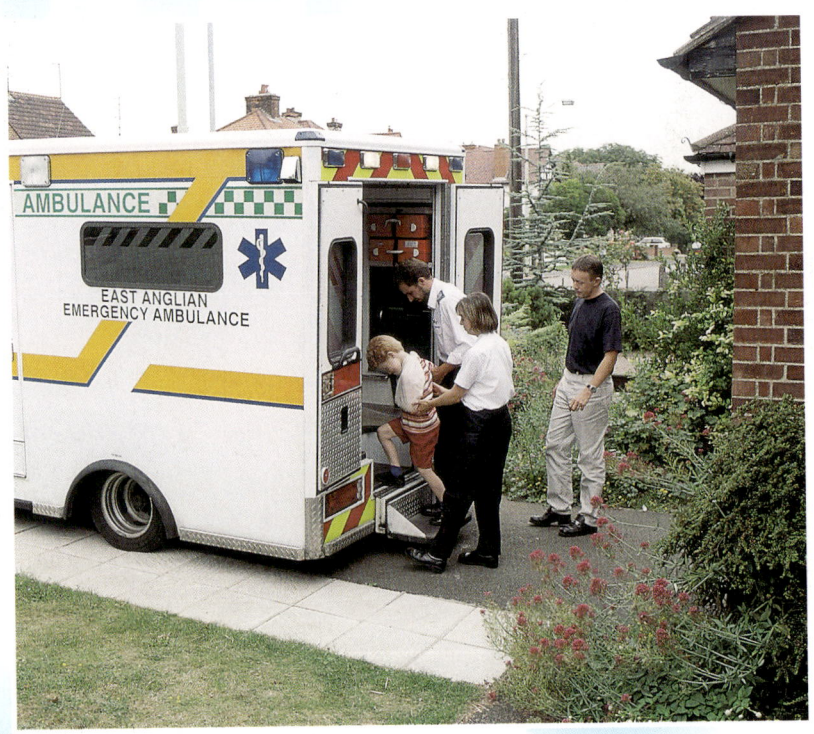

An ambulance came.

I went to the hospital.

# At the hospital

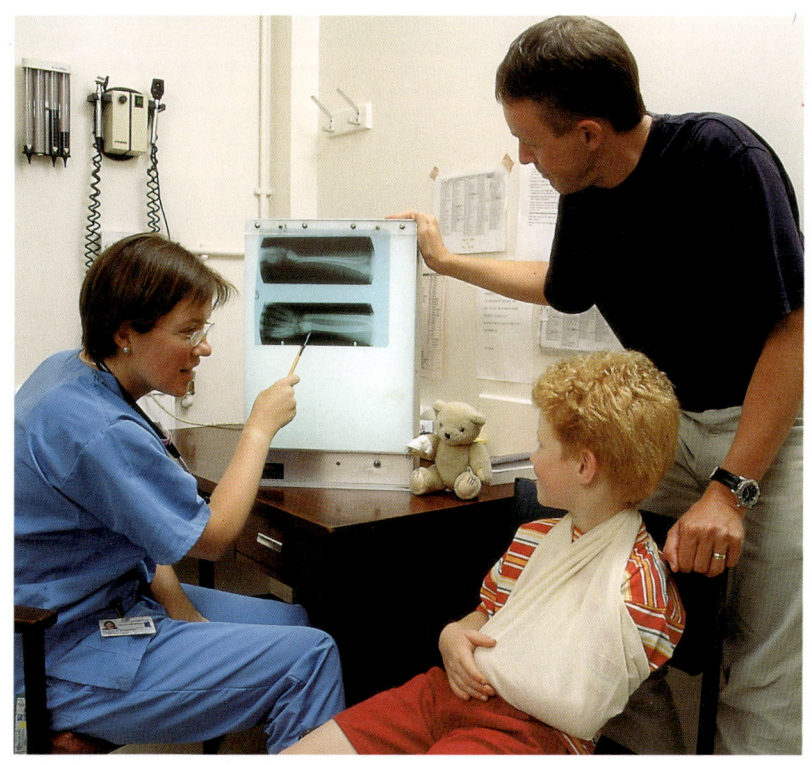

I had an X-ray.

The nurse put my arm in plaster.

# Six weeks later

I'm better now.